# WRITE ON TARGET

# WRITE ON TARGET

## Sue Spencer

WORD BOOKS, PUBLISHER
Waco, Texas

All Scripture quotations, unless otherwise noted, are from the Revised Standard Version of the Bible, copyrighted 1946, 1952, © 1971, 1973 by the Division of Christian Education of the National Council of the Churches of Christ in the U.S.A., and are used by permission.

ISBN 0-87680-880-1
Library of Congress catalog card number: 75-36193
Printed in the United States of America

ILLUSTRATIONS BY DENNIS HILL

# *Acknowledgments*

Grateful acknowledgment is made for the use of copyrighted material from: *Looking Back: A Chronicle of Growing Up Old in the Sixties* by Joyce Maynard, copyright © 1972, 1973 by Joyce Maynard, used by permission of Doubleday & Company; *Ella Price's Journal* by Dorothy Bryant, copyright © 1972 by Dorothy Bryant, reprinted by permission of J. B. Lippincott Company; *An Antique Drum* by Thomas Howard, copyright © 1969 by Thomas T. Howard, reprinted by permission of J. B. Lippincott Company; *Gift of the Unicorn: Essays on Writing* by Percival Hunt by permission of the University of Pittsburgh Press, © 1965 by the University of Pittsburgh Press; *Nobel Lecture* by Alexander Solzhenitsyn, translated by F. D. Reeve, © 1972 The Nobel Foundation, English Translation copyright © 1972 by Farrar, Straus & Giroux, Inc.; a review by Philip Rosenberg of *Emile Durkheim: His Life and Work* in the *New York Times* of July 15, 1973, © 1973 by the New York Times Company, reprinted by permission; *A Psychology of Nothingness* by William F. Kraft, copyright © 1974, The Westminster Press, used by permission; *The Female Eunuch*

# Acknowledgments

by Germaine Greer, copyright 1971 by Germaine Greer, used with permission of McGraw-Hill Book Company; *Return the Innocent Earth* by Wilma Dykeman, copyright © 1973 by Wilma Dykeman, reprinted by permission of Holt, Rinehart and Winston, Publishers; *The Modern Stylists: Writers on the Art of Writing* by Donald Hall, copyright © 1968 by Donald Hall, used by permission of Macmillan Publishing Co., Inc.; *We Have This Treasure* by Paul Scherer, copyright © 1944 by Harper & Brothers, used by permission of Harper & Row, Publishers; *Future Shock* by Alvin Toffler, copyright © 1970 by Alvin Toffler, used by permission of Random House, Inc.; *When the Saints Go Marching Out* by Charles Merrill Smith, copyright © 1969 by Charles Merrill Smith, used by permission of Doubleday & Co.; *How to Be Your Own Best Friend* by Mildred Newman and Bernard Berkowitz, copyright © 1973 by Mildred Newman and Bernard Berkowitz, used by permission of Random House, Inc.; and *Gift from the Sea* by Anne Morrow Lindbergh, copyright © 1955 by Anne Morrow Lindbergh, used by permission of Random House, Inc.

# Contents

# BONER'S ARK By Addison

Conveying truth . . . is not as simple as we imagine. Given its elusive nature and the restless audience we confront, . . . we need to know how to produce material short enough to attract and hold busy, distracted people which does not, at the same time, sacrifice truth.

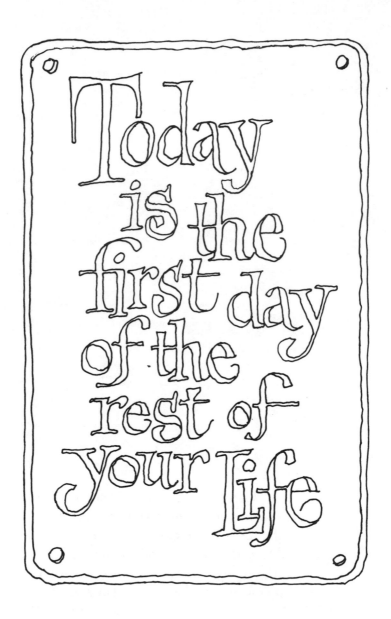

*1.*

# Know the Score

Posters used to announce when the PTA would meet. Today they teach anthropology, give psychiatric advice and substitute for Sunday sermons. Everyone's communication cup is running over. We are bombarded with some 20,000 sell messages every day! In order to exist, we have had to foreshorten and simplify everything.

Such posters as the one on the opposite page represent all the "philosophy" many people can or will ever take. A communicator can no longer count on a steadily involved audience. Listen to eighteen-year-old Joyce Maynard in her *Chronicle of Growing Up Old in the Sixties:*

> I can't say that none of us read books, but certainly we weren't a Generation of Readers. We never *had* to read—there was always TV. . . . Once accustomed to television, we were impatient with book dramas: they moved so slowly, took so much effort, required us to visualize things and cluttered the story, as I saw it then, with the superfluous details writers put in only to please English teachers. I skipped over the descriptions of people's eyes or their sitting rooms or the sunsets they walked through, moving instead straight to the action, which could never compete with what I got watching "Highway Patrol" and "Wagon Train."[1]

### Our message is important!

This, then, is our communication situation. We are one voice among many vying for attention. We have no captive audience. We strive to reach people who are impatient, distracted, busy. Although they have deliberately tuned us in or traveled a distance to attend our lecture or paid money for our book, they will not necessarily hear us out. Like a surgeon facing a malignancy, they are poised to scrape away whatever threatens to be dull, irrelevant or hokey; whatever writers "put in to please English teachers" or preachers put in to please theology professors!

14

What a quandary this poses! Most of us have messages that require, we think, thoughtful consideration on the part of the listener/reader. We are not selling soap or cereal. Our material is more important, more complicated and more interconnected. We are drafting policy statements, explaining contracts, outlining procedures; we are setting forth eternal principles, sounding great alarms or beating the drum for some vital cause. What we're trying to communicate, by its very nature, demands time and length. It certainly won't fit on a poster. What are we to do?

## The whole truth?

At the heart of our qaundary lies our commitment to truth. We don't want to shortchange it. We think of truth as the point-by-point correlation between what-is-said-about-a-reality and the reality itself. If, for example, we are giving an account of "what happened," we tell exactly what took place in precisely the order in which it took place. The minutes of our meetings include everything from the opening gavel to the delicious refreshments served by Mrs. So-and-So. We omit nothing. We reproduce conversations word for word. We do not think of the descriptions of people's eyes or their sitting rooms or the sunsets they walked through as superfluous.

We are equally exacting when it comes to non-narrative prose. If there are two sides to a question, we feel honor-bound to expose them both. If there are four possible explanations for a matter, we set down all four. If there are six factors to be considered, we give six, no less. And, of course, all sermons *must* have at least three points. Whatever we are communicating, we strive to make our words and the reality coincide exactly and totally.

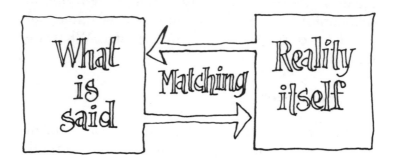

### Alternatives

Given this pedestrian concept of truth, we seem to face only two alternatives, both unsatisfactory. On the one hand, we can go ahead, tell the whole reality and run the risk of never being heard; in effect, give up on the "poster generation" and keep on grinding out our lengthy messages. If someone asks us, at some future date, to give an accounting of our communicating efforts, we can claim that we did our part; we put forth (or down) the message faithfully, making it available to the public. We can't help it if people didn't heed it. The water was there for the horse to drink; we cannot be blamed that it galloped away!

On the other hand we can report less than the whole story and get a hearing, possibly. But in so doing, we run the risk of failing to "do right by" truth. By not spreading out before our readers or audience the full story, we may communicate a half-truth or a lie. A jokester once pointed out that Jesus said, "Hang all the law and the prophets!" He did, but his total sentence in Matthew 22:40, King James Version, was: "On these two commandments [love God and your neighbor] *hang all the law and the prophets.*" Because we abhor this kind of misrepresentation we are reluctant to leave anything out of our messages.

### Reality is elusive

But what if truth is not as pedestrian as we have imagined? Suppose it has dimensions we've overlooked. Suppose it has elusive qualities that, at times, cannot be captured by means of "accurate" or "objective" words or be welded indelibly to a page. Suppose, even, that there are occasions when the slavish reproduction of reality actually *befogs* truth. Take, for example, the alerts sent to Pearl Harbor just prior to the 1941 attack. On November 27, Army Headquarters in Washington sent this cablegram to the army commander:

> Negotiations with Japanese appear to be
> terminated to all practical purposes, with only the
> barest possibility that the Japanese government
> might come back and offer to continue. Japanese
> future action unpredictable, but hostile action
> possible at any moment. If hostility cannot,
> repeat cannot, be avoided, the U.S. desires that
> Japan commit the first overt act. Prior to hostile
> Japanese action, you are directed to undertake
> such reconnaissance and other measures as you
> deem necessary but these measures should be
> carried out so as not, repeat not, to alarm civil
> population or disclose intent.

On the same day, the Navy sent a cablegram to the naval commander that read:

> Consider this a warning of war!

Because of a degree of cooperation between the armed services, both commanders got both cablegrams. And both gave more credence to the one from Army Head-quarters. It was, after all, a factual report of what was going on in Washington; it offered a point-by-point correlation with the negotiating realities. Yet, in retrospect, we can see that the Navy message told THE truth. A prediction—tied to no reality, and yet tied to the very reality that needed to be conveyed. Words which didn't match anything but, in the end, encompassed everything!

18      Conveying truth, then, is not as simple as we imag-

ine. Given its elusive nature and the restless audience we confront, we desperately need a third alternative. We need to know how to produce material short enough to attract and hold busy, distracted people which does not, at the same time, sacrifice truth. The rest of this book deals with that alternative, describing the principles and methods of effective modern communication. I invite you to read on . . .

Do you have an idea or truth you want to get across? Thump on it. Sift it through in your mind. Take soundings along its borders. See if there isn't some part that, properly developed, will communicate the rest of it, . . . that will accurately reflect the texture and substance of the whole.

# 2.

## Bite Off What You Can Chew

Suppose that I have a large, complicated message I want to get across, but I haven't been allowed as much time or space as I think is needed. What happens?

Usually I begin by letting the audience know this insufficiency: I mention the "brief time allotted" or say something about struggling to condense my vast subject into a few pages. By so doing I render the already-too-small time/space even smaller; but this result I ignore. For I *must* stave off the charge—practically the worst that could be leveled—that I have *oversimplified!*

Then I proceed with my topic. The History of Great Movements. Scientific Concepts and Their Ramifications. Democratic Political Issues. The World of the Arts. Having saddled myself with some such enormity, I am restricted to generalities. I can hit only the high spots because there isn't any room to drop down and elaborate or give a "f'r instance."

### Selling the watermelon

I would do better to learn a lesson from my local produce vendor. He has a watermelon for sale and therein a dilemma. He wants to demonstrate the condition of the whole big thing, but he can't afford to part with it. So, after due thumpings, he plunges a knife into what he estimates to be a typical spot. From it he extracts a plug, vibrant with the colors, juiciness, texture and taste of all the rest. This, and this alone, he uses to convince his customers.

Too many communicators stick to the total melon. They are determined to foist the whole thing on their customers *regardless;* they believe the only way to transfer a reality is to transfer a reality. So, beginning at some far end of their subject, they start peeling. Round and round they go, but all I get is handfuls of shallow rind. Before they've ever arrived at the "heart" of their subject, any reader/listener

24

has tuned them out. Here is a missionary telling in a letter about her life as a superintendent of teachers in a South American country:

In the town of [name], a Sunday School has been held among the adults in the house of a Christian family. However, a vacation Bible school brought in many children making it necessary to have a regular Sunday school for the children also. This was managed by an earlier hour on Sunday afternoon so that there would be sufficient time to reach the other Sunday school in [town name].

The Sunday school in [town name] was begun in the middle of [year] in the home of an interested family. Within a few months the enrollment of children had increased to the point that it was necessary to rent a house in order to have sufficient room.

The school ran smoothly during [year]. I have truly felt God's guidance and help in meeting the many tasks that the supervision of schools demands and in the good relationships with the teachers. However at the end of the year the region had to close the schools due to insufficient funds. The churches have assumed responsibility of the schools. In [town] the city has promised a subvention for teachers' salaries. In [town] the tuition was raised in an effort to maintain the school.

The writer is trying to send us a whole year of her life in just three paragraphs. The colors, the juices, 25

the textures and tastes of her experiences never sur-
face. *How* has God helped to guide her? In what specifics? What demands did her position put upon her?
In what ways were her good relationships with the
teachers threatened? How were the threats resolved?
Determined to cover such a long time span, she has
no space for the interesting details. All she offers is a
quick succession of blurred, vague pictures. How
much better to write fully of just *one* way God helped
her. Or fully of *one* school in *one* town. Suppose she
had carefully reconstructed one of her conversations
with a Latin teacher, a conversation that would reflect the kinds of problems they regularly worked out
together.

See what a difference we get in this tightly orga-
nized paragraph from Antoine de Saint-Exupéry's
*Wind, Sand and Stars:*

One day, on the Madrid front, I chanced upon a
school that stood on a hill surrounded by a low
stone wall some five hundred yards behind the
trenches. A corporal was teaching botany that day.
He was lecturing on the fragile organs of a poppy
held in his hands. Out of the surrounding mud,
and in spite of the wandering shells that dropped
all about, he had drawn like a magnet an audience
of stubble-bearded soldiers who squatted tailor
fashion and listened with their chins in their
hands to a discourse of which they understood
not a word in five. Something within them had
said: "You are but brutes fresh from your caves.

Go along! Catch up with humanity!" And they had hurried on their muddy clogs to overtake it.[1]

## Tackle but a part

Do you have an idea or truth you want to get across? Thump on it. Sift it through your mind. Take soundings along its borders. See if there isn't some part that, properly developed, will communicate the rest of it—some part that will accurately reflect the texture and substance of the whole. When you've found it, take on *this* rather than the whole. Since you will have many less generalities to deal with, you will be able to develop each point with care rather than stumbling frantically from one to the next.

When Alexander Solzhenitsyn wanted to convey the idea of "The Triumph of the Human Spirit over Totalitarianism" he wrote, instead, *One Day in the Life of Ivan Denisovich.* And what happened? As Ivan Denisovich's day unfolded before us, we beheld the triumph of the human spirit over totalitarianism. When Bel Kaufman wanted to expose the frustrating administrative machinery that burdens teachers today, she wrote *Up the Down Staircase.* She did not write "Education versus Bureaucratic Red Tape." Or did she? In actuality, the sign about which she wrote (*Don't go up the down staircase*) caught the very essence of it.

27

So if you are toying with a lecture on "Humanity in a Technological World," you may do better by considering "John Doe and Computer 602." If you want to tell something about "The Impact of Electronic Media on the Young," you may get it across more effectively by handling "Mary Lou Watches Sesame Street." If you're blocking out a book on urban problems, the preservation of wildlife or the history of the American Indians, why not rethink the scope of your project? You are probably biting off more than you can chew. You may expose all urban problems more urgently and forcefully by portraying those of only one city. And you will probably do more for ecology by sticking to one endangered species, or for the American Indian by sticking to one tribe.

### Asking for trouble

Ministers who preach on such subjects as "The Pauline Doctrine of Justification," "Dynamic Imperatives for Ecumenicity," "Christological Concepts in the New Testament" and "The Messianic Prophecies of the Pentateuch" are asking for trouble. They are condemning themselves *in advance* to a dull, lifeless procedure.

I recently heard a communion meditation lasting ten minutes in which the minister tried to cover all three aspects of the traditional monastic vow. That's

less than four minutes devoted to obedience;
less than four minutes devoted to poverty;
less than four minutes devoted to chastity!

## Choose a modest topic

If you are given a ten-minute time slot on a program, deal with a ten-minute topic. If you are challenged to tell something in twenty-five words or less, choose a twenty-five-words-or-less subject. Jesus covered "friendship" in the story of the Good Samaritan (151 words!). The subject need contain only the essence. If it does, we the readers/listeners will grasp the whole. I once knew a woman who was asked to describe modern Japan in one sentence. She said, "Japan is a country filled with people who are unfailingly polite except when getting on the subways at rush hour!" The essence . . . the whole.

Choose, then, a modest topic. An amenable topic. One that you can truly handle in the time/space afforded.

Beginnings can make or break.
Many a manuscript is rejected by a publisher,
many a TV channel is changed, and many a
speech goes unheeded because of a
slow or uninteresting start.

# 3.

# Get Off

# to a Flying Start

Movie producer Billy Wilder understands the importance of good beginnings. He says:

In Europe, you can shoot clouds. Then more clouds. Then still more clouds. For an American audience you photograph the clouds once and it is done. Next time you show clouds, you have to have an airplane. And if you show the clouds a third time, you have to show that plane explode or the audience wraps up the popcorn and goes home![1]

Beginnings can make or break. Many a manuscript is rejected by a publisher, many a TV channel is changed, and many a speech goes unheeded because of a slow or uninteresting start.

### Don't start too far back

Communicators often begin too far back, *before* their genuine beginning. They feel obliged to forage up a lot of tedious "background." It isn't necessary. You don't have to tell everything that led up to what you want to say. You seldom have to locate your material in its historical setting. In short, you don't need to imitate the French newsman who, having witnessed the burning of Paris in 1621, began his account:

> God whose goodness and clemencie is incomprehensible, to our humane thoughts and imaginations, doth not always discharge the sorrows of his wrath upon miserable sinners; who have stirred up and provoked his wrath against them. But when he seeth that they waxe worse, hardened in their sinnes, then he rouzeth up himselfe with the scourge of adversitie and dischargeth the fury of his wrath against them, to make them turn unto him. Then (I say) he employeth the great forces of heaven and the elements, thereby to heale the vicer of their vices . . .[2]

Eventually he gets to the fire and the estimate of the smoke and water damage from the insurance adjusters!

Here's what often happens. Dan Collins started out an essay:

> Only five weeks ago he introduced himself to me. Already he has become the most exciting person I've ever met. Because he means so much to me, I cannot resist acquainting you with my son, Dan.

Does there follow a description of a wiggling, beguiling baby, making its way in its new world? No, there follows a paragraph in which Dan learns that his wife *is going to have the baby*. Then comes a paragraph in which he takes his wife to the hospital for the birth. In the third paragraph, he basks in a postbirth period of awe and pride. Eventually he gets the child home and tells us a little bit about it. But at the end of the essay I feel much more acquainted with Dan, Sr. than Dan, Jr.

What happened? The writer began before his beginning. He started much too far back in the experience. Then, holding generally to the concept of truth as a point-by-point correlation with reality, he couldn't just leapfrog over the intervening events. So he slogged on through them as best he could, hitting the high spots. In the end, they absorbed so much of his energy and space that he never got around to telling us what he intended to.

35

### Begin at your beginning

So begin at *your* beginning—at the point closest to your real interest. Take Mark in the New Testament, for example. He liked action, so the on-the-move, hurried, harried Jesus fascinated him. He launches his gospel with John the Baptist preaching in the wilderness, giving us no more introduction than "the beginning of the gospel of Jesus Christ, the Son of God." No theological setting a là John with "in the beginning was the Word." No sociological setting à la Matthew with "the genealogy of Jesus Christ, the son of David, the son of Abraham." No historical setting à la Luke with Caesar Augustus, Mary, Joseph, the angels, shepherds and all the rest. Let others tell where Jesus came from and how he got here; Mark starts at *his* beginning.

### What and how

In your introduction try to do two things: tell the people what they are about to experience and help them understand why they should go ahead with it. Alvin Toffler begins *Future Shock:*

> In the three decades between now and the twenty-first century, millions of ordinary, psychologically normal people will face an abrupt collision with the future. Citizens of the world's richest and most technically advanced nations,

many of them, will find it increasingly painful to keep up with the incessant demand for change that characterizes our time. For them, the future will have arrived too soon.

This book is about change and how we adapt to it.[3]

Great! He has told us what we are about to read. On the very next page he continues:

Much that now strikes us as incomprehensible would be far less so if we took a fresh look at the racing rate of change that makes reality seem, sometimes, like a kaleidoscope run wild. For the acceleration of change does not merely buffet industries or nations. It is a concrete force that reaches deep into our personal lives, compels us to act out new roles, and confronts us with the danger of a new and powerfully upsetting psychological disease. This new disease can be called "future shock," and a knowledge of its sources and symptoms helps explain many things that otherwise defy rational analysis.[4]

Splendid! In the space of a few paragraphs, we now know enough to judge whether or not we want (or need) to read the rest.

But suppose Mr. Toffler had begun, instead, something like this:

Before we can understand the future, we must first understand the past. Before we can comprehend the complexities created by our technology, we must examine the nature of the changes that occurred during the industrial revolution. Before we can grasp the enormous transitions that are affecting the structures of our institutions and governments, we must first try to . . .

Would you continue? I doubt it!

## The tough stuff

Is the message you're trying to get across unpopular? unbelievable? in any way hard to swallow? Is it coming to the reader/listener unbidden or apt to arrive at an inopportune time? The higher the hurdles it must leap, the greater the imperative to present the what and why. Charles Merrill Smith reckons accurately with the odds when he begins *When the Saints Go Marching Out:*

> On the face of it nothing could be of less use to the man of the computer age than a study of the lives of the saints. The saints instruct the pious in ways and means of putting the heat on heaven to let a chap in, methods of extracting approval from the Almighty (apparently not easily come by), and other payoffs for proper religious conduct. But will a careful perusal of St. Vindicianus of Bullecourt show a fellow how to turn a fast buck? Can a chapter a night from the biography of St. Theophanes the Chronographer help us cope with

crabgrass? Of course not, you say. But you would be wrong.

It is our intent to demonstrate how you can get that promotion, grab off the cash, win the game by the employment of lessons learned from the lives of the saints. You no doubt think this an unlikely claim, but keep reading.[5]

If you are telling a story or giving a narrative account of an event, start at some dramatic, gripping point. Do this even if there is mundane material that must eventually come to light. (It can be introduced by means of a flashback or a reminiscence.) Begin by piquing curiosity, with action à la Hans Kirst:

Grenadier Recht flung open the window and leaped into the night [First sentence in *What Became of Gunner Asch?*].[6]

with intrigue à la Frederick Forsyth:

It is cold at 6:40 in the morning of a March day in Paris, and it seems even colder when a man is about to be executed by firing squad [First sentence in *The Day of the Jackal*].[7]

or with promising conversation à la P. G. Wodehouse:

"Corky, Old Horse," said Stanley Featherstonehaugh Ukridge, in a stunned voice, "this is the most amazing thing I have heard in the whole course of my existence. I'm astounded. You could knock me down with a feather." [8]

Wade in arbitrarily. Begin at your beginning. The past, the prologue, the what-preceded can become whirlpools, sucking you into never-ending explanations, never-ending attempts to fill in the gaps. A child need not be traced back to the moment of conception; a fire can be reported without stretching back to "God whose goodness and clemencie is incomprehensible"! Take hold of your topic at the place where it takes hold of you.

No one sees further into a
generalization than his own knowledge
of the details extends.

—*William James*

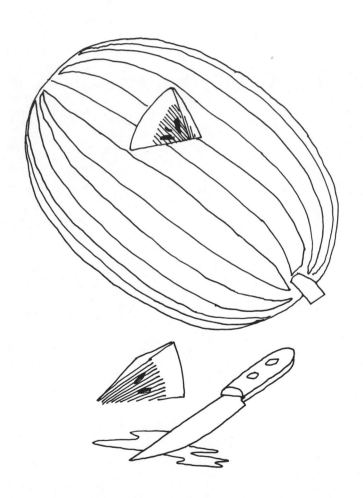

# 4.

# Zero In

Zero in on your narrowed topic. Give us a close-up, sharp and clear. The colors, the juices, the texture—all. Set before us those details we must see if we are to be enlightened or persuaded. In an article in *Newsweek*, Paul Zimmerman says, "Art is best when it arrives at general truths through the observation of concrete detail." He then goes on to criticize a movie that "starts from the wrong end—with an elaborate scheme—and shuts out all the convincing specifics that make art believable." *

## The fatigue factor

Our natural inclination is to tell a little about a lot. When we first set out to communicate something, we want to cover the whole thing and cover it, if possible, quickly. We especially want to zip past the dull parts (those pre-beginnings we insist on embracing) in order to get to what really interests us. We saddle ourselves with much too much and in trying to handle it, fatigue, rather than skill, becomes our winnower.

The missionary in chapter 2 who wanted to ship us her entire last year in one letter wrote four sentences (A, B, C, D) about the school situation in one town. She thought of telling more, but in the fourth sentence she had already mentioned the school in town two. And she still had several others to cover. She had better move on. So she decided to skip town two (maybe E, F, G and H) and go ahead with three (I, J, K and L). By the time she finished with three, she was tiring of the process itself. She still had spiritual and financial matters she must get to. So she simply collected everything up in a vague, catch-all

sentence: "The schools ran smoothly during [year]."
(M through T, all jammed together!)

Plan and purpose do not guide what is put down
and what is left out; fatigue does—a fatigue born out
of the intimidating assignment the writer gave herself. Such communication leaves the recipient un-
satisfied and skeptical. Here is how a reviewer for
the *Washington Post* reacted to the idea of group
marriage after reading a book aimed at *selling* it:

> . . . they [the authors] provide no case histories,
> and no undoctored examples of any of the be-
> havior they discuss, no vivid or plausible docu-
> mentation, but only pages and pages of
> incredibly dull, laboriously defensive argument
> which somehow insists on the validity of group
> marriage despite the contradictory evidence of
> even their heavily bowdlerized material. After
> reading this report, it is unlikely that anyone
> would be moved to set up a triad, pentad or
> heptad.[1]

## A lot about a little

What we should do is tell a lot about a little; delve
into our narrowed topic intensely. We see the difference in an episode from *Ella Price's Journal*. It
concerns a young housewife who enrolls in a nearby
junior college. One of her classes is English, and her
principal assignment in that class is to keep a diary
for the semester. The story consists of her entries, one

45

by one. As the months pass, we watch her learn how to communicate.

Her first entry on Wednesday, September 21, reads:

> I am taking three subjects at Bay Junior College —English, psychology and social science.
> Today I got up early, got Joe off to work and Lulu off to school, and cleaned up the house a little before going to psychology. I studied in the library until my English class. Tonight I made Joe's favorite dinner, steak and baked potato, with apple pie for dessert.[2]

She decided to tell about her whole day and it was a mistake; fatigue began setting in almost as soon as she got up! Her hop, skip and jump through the hours reveals that she has a husband and a daughter, but gives us none of the flavor of her life and personality.

**Learn to cover less**

Thirty-three entries later she has learned to zero in on a much smaller segment and tell it with intensity:

> No school today. Yesterday was Thanksgiving. It was a mess. I got into an argument with my brother-in-law about the war. Was I stupid! I could have avoided it, but I was too busy showing off what I'd learned in the reading I did for my

social science class. But I wasn't just showing off; I was sincere. The things I read were so different from what I had heard—well, I thought that all I had to do was tell him these things and, hearing them, he'd want to read those books too and find out all these facts that were left out of the newspapers. But it didn't matter what I told him; he didn't want his ideas shaken. He started yelling all kinds of stupid things and ended up by saying that a couple of months in college had turned me into a smart-alecky Communist and he'd stick to the things he knew in his heart, no matter how anybody tried to confuse him.

I looked around the table at everyone to see their reaction to this. I expected them to laugh, or at least look at him like the fool he was, but they were all looking at me as a trouble-maker. Even Joe kept looking at his plate as if he were ashamed of me—Lulu was too—so I shut up.

Then Joe began joking. He told his old Army joke—I guess to make everyone forget how awkward I'd made things—and soon everything was back to normal.[3]

Here is one meal. No, not even the whole meal: she confines herself almost exclusively to the exchanges between herself and her brother-in-law. She doesn't abbreviate the conversation in any way or succumb to summary. She gives it all. She can afford to reconstruct the incident line by line, because this is the only one she has taken on and it doesn't threaten her with exhaustion.

As Ella proceeds with her journal, she tells more

about less. And as she does, she really tells *more* about *more*. We know not only that she has a husband and daughter, we know something of her relationship to them and theirs to her. We also know what is happening to that relationship as a result of what is happening to Ella. The "plugs" that she carves out of her existence run with the juices and pulsate with the essence of her life.

**Apply the technique creatively**

At this point you may be cheering Ella on and, at the same time, rejecting her method for yourself. "It's okay for narrative stuff," you may be saying, "but I deal with something very different." Maybe you are trying to communicate company policies, ecological problems or theological truths. It doesn't matter. Unless held in check, our natural inclinations will prevail. We will stumble from one enormous, unexplored point to another. Here is a Christian educator writing a committee report about "the crisis in education":

> The crisis is religious and theological. In the face of the image given by science of the nature of the universe, the growing knowledge about man and the dehumanization of a technological society, the credibility and vitality of the Christian faith has been greatly weakened. Consequently the churches have seriously fallen behind in their role of nourishing the vital centers of personal and

social decision-making, encouraging genuine humane concern for persons, providing resources of personal security that must underlie ethical and moral commitment, and giving us a vision of a meaningful life and future to which mankind may aspire.

So far as technique is concerned, this paragraph is just like Ella Price's first entry. Both writers are skipping from topic sentence to topic sentence without pausing to develop any one of them. Ms. Price said, "I am taking English." Her next sentence should have been something like, "We are studying the Romantic poets" or "The teacher intrigues me." Instead she rushes on to psychology.

The Christian educator said, "The crisis is religious and theological." His next sentences should have established unmistakably the link or links between religion and education. Instead he begins exploring the erosion of faith and the church. As he proceeds, he introduces such gargantuan topics and wanders so far from anything that I can immediately relate to education that the whole thrust is lost. "No one," says William James, "sees further into a generalization than his own knowledge of the details extends."

Suppose that early in the game the educator had shown me how, in some concrete way, the church's "giving us a vision of meaningful life, etc., etc." aided education in the past. Then, when he an-

**49**

nounced later on, that the church, because of the erosion that has taken place, can no longer provide such a vision, I would grasp the point.

## Take your receivers along

The educator, alas, is telling me too little about too much. He is leaving out connections (probably plain to him) in order to cover his vast subject. But he isn't taking the reader along. He is, in effect, forcing me to look through a telescope without extending its sections; little wonder I don't see what he does.

In contrast, see how, in her book *The Edge of the Sea,* Rachel Carson sticks to the edge of the sea but at the same time keeps spreading it out before us:

> The edge of the sea is a strange and beautiful place. All through the long history of Earth it has been an area of unrest where waves have broken heavily against the land, where the tides have pressed forward over the continents, receded, and then returned. For no two successive days is the shoreline precisely the same. Not only do the tides advance and retreat in their eternal rhythms, but the level of the sea itself is never at rest. It rises or falls as the glaciers melt or grow, as the floor of the deep ocean basins shifts under its increasing load of sediments, or as the earth's crust along the continental margins warps up or down in adjustment to strain and tension. Today

a little more land may belong to the sea, tomorrow
a little less. Always the edge of the sea remains
an elusive and indefinable boundary.[4]

After you have reduced your topic to a manageable
size, zoom in on it. Give us the "wedge" or "plug" of
your truth in all its completeness. Tell us a lot about
a little.

Does my opening contain bait? Will it provoke curiosity? Does it hint at the opening of some vista? Does it relate to the potential hearer/reader in such a way that he will be intrigued and want to continue?

# 5.

## Keep

## Dropping Those

## Bread Crumbs

Readers and listeners need to have a sense that they're getting somewhere. There must be something to follow. An incident that unfolds. Facts set down in such a way that they enlighten. A truth that becomes increasingly clearer. A sequence that can be ticked off. A mystery that unravels. A tension that builds and dissolves. In short, there must be a sense of movement.

When people don't get it, watch out! Here's a

reader venting his spleen in the book review section of the *Washington Post:*

> The mind works peculiarly. There is nothing quite so appealing to it as the opportunity to make connections—this bit of information fitting in here, this event following that one—all meaning precisely . . . what? Yes, that is the problem with *Gravity's Rainbow*. It offers the promise of a pattern where none exists. A novel that gives us so many clues, that purports to tell us about so many things in its hyped-up, self-important, everything-is-everything style actually and finally tells us nothing at all![1]

## Too much freight

One way to retard movement is to load too much freight into each sentence. In a welter of words, the couplings drop away. The reader/listener gets bogged down and forgets the overall thrust. (Often the communicator does too!) Here is a paragraph that appeared on a church bulletin cover:

> We have the obligation to restore to our fellowman his personal worth and dignity as a human being. The society in which we live puts more value on property than on humans. We hold within us the "Good News" that God came to us in Jesus Christ to assure us of our importance as persons. Our responsibility is, by word and deed, to let all men know that they

are children of God, loved and wanted by him.

I trust you have already noticed that the writer is struggling with enormous topics. He has produced heavy, hulking, declarative sentences with no readily recognizable sequential order. What difference does it make if I substitute sentence one for sentence four? Or two for three? Or three for one or four for two?

> We hold within us the "Good News" that God came to us in Jesus Christ to assure us of our importance as persons. Our responsibility is, by word and deed, to let all men know that they are children of God, loved and wanted by him. The society in which we live puts more value on property than on humans. We have the obligation to restore to our fellowman his personal worth and dignity as a human being.

You can, in fact, put the four sentences together in *any* combination (2, 4, 1, 3; 3, 1, 4, 2, etc.) and still not get anywhere, because each sentence tells everything. There is no suspense, nothing to egg the reader on from one piece of information to the next. There is nothing for the reader to do. He can agree or disagree, but there is no obvious thread of thought for him to follow from an embryonic stage through to the end. And that's precisely what he likes to do. Mark Hellinger says the communicator should be the eyes, ears and nose of the reader: *"the reader is his own brain!"*

## Writing that moves

Consider in contrast this paragraph from Thomas Howard's *An Antique Drum:*

> But this soup can. It seems banality, if not an obscenity, next to this Vermeer. If he is going to turn our attention to food at all, couldn't the artist have chosen an oil cruet, perhaps, or a pepper mill, or at least a Chianti bottle? Something with an interesting shape, and some texture, that would evoke for us the world of fine cuisine? Why this stark commercialism? We come to the gallery to get *away* from the A&P. After all, we are in there almost every morning of our lives. It is a bore to be hailed by a large intransigent soup can here. It is slightly jolting, most certainly depressing, and, after a bit, alarming. The initial cackle of amusement flickers off into the quavering heh-hehs of the man who finds that the funny person in the mask is the executioner after all.[2]

How satisfying! The paragraph moves, carrying me along. At the end I see more than I did at the beginning. I have had a mini-revelation. I still don't see all, because there's more to come. This paragraph appears on page 83 in a chapter that ends on page 95 in a book that ends on page 157. Revealing, unfolding, elucidating continues all along the way. On page 157 the vision rounds out and I see most fully, but not until then. This is paced communication.

The writer's prose displays several characteristics typical of writing that moves. Thomas is already dealing with a modest subject: a person's reaction to finding a painting of a soup can in an art gallery. He does not hesitate to omit subjects and predicates where the sense of what he's saying is retained without them and where to include them would simply slow the reader's progress. "But this soup can" has meaning in its context without any accompanying verb. "Why doesn't the artist paint" need not precede "something with an interesting shape. . . ."

Many of his sentences begin with pronouns, which is significant. It indicates that the writer isn't introducing new topics; he is instead dealing intensely with the one already under discussion. Also, he isn't repeating the noun (the topic), because this both slows the reader and demeans his intelligence. If you're talking about "the problem" and you begin every sentence with "the problem," you create kindergarten prose.

Furthermore, pronouns by their very throwback nature bespeak connectedness. They indicate that what has already been said about the subject isn't all there is to be said, thus luring the reader along to hear the matter out.

Finally you will notice that the writer varies the *kinds* of sentences he uses; they aren't all declarative. How often in a single phrase questions and exclamations relay information that declarative sen-

**59**

tences can transmit only by means of long, wordy explanations!

### Several key questions

Now, obviously, leaving out subjects and predicates willy-nilly, strewing our paragraphs with pronouns and mixing up the kinds of sentences we use will not, per se, guarantee beckoning prose. But they are clues. They need to be augmented by asking several questions.

Does (or will) my opening contain bait? Will it provoke curiosity? Does it hint at the opening of some vista? Does it relate to the potential hearer/reader in such a way that he will be intrigued and want to continue?

I once worked with a committee that was interested in making a survey. We devised a questionnaire to send out to busy ministers, and one of our committee members composed a letter to go with it. It began:

> When ecumenical thought and work are in evidence at the grass roots, national and international efforts may become more relevant.

Wouldn't you file that in the wastebasket? Why not something like:

> You can help the ecumenical work of your synod by devoting a few minutes to this letter.

Do you remember how *Future Shock* begins? (We referred to it in chapter 3.) The author mentions his potential reader repeatedly. In the first sentence he speaks of "millions of ordinary, psychologically normal people." That's me the reader, unless I'm willing to confess that I'm not psychologically normal! In the second sentence, Toffler talks of the "citizens of the world's richest and most technically advanced nations" and in sentence three, to "them."

Just as he keeps referring to the reader, he keeps warning what is about to happen to him/her. "Normal people," he says, "will face an abrupt collision with the future." The citizens of advanced nations "will find it increasingly painful to keep up with the incessant demand for change." I the reader am in danger; I must read on.

Then on the next page the author identifies my danger as "future shock" and assures me that "a knowledge of its sources and symptoms helps explain many things that otherwise defy analysis." So, unless I understand everything (and who does!) I must continue reading. Mr. Toffler is dropping bread crumbs all along the way. As long as he does, I'll follow his trail.

Which brings us to another question we need to ask about our communication: does it digress from the point or thrust? Remember what Joyce Maynard said in our first chapter: "I skipped over the descriptions of people's eyes or their sitting rooms or the

61

sunsets they walked through, moving straight to the action"? If you think that eyes or rooms or sunsets are not detours, you're still in a pre-TV era.

The link that one element has to another (a sunset to the action) needs to be very clear or we *appear* to digress. In chapter 4 we looked at two paragraphs that began with the same structure:

| | |
|---|---|
| The crisis [in education] is religious and theological. | The edge of the sea is strange and beautiful. |

The subject of the second sentence about the sea is "it" because Ms. Carson is still talking about the same thing. The subject of the second sentence about the crisis in education is "the credibility and vitality of the Christian faith." This is both a new topic and one that is hard to find, because it comes after three heavily freighted phrases. It is the first step in a series that will eventually expose the religious/theological dimensions of the crisis. Here is the progression the writer intended:

1) something has happened to the Christian faith
2) as a result, something has happened to the church
3) as a result of what has happened to the church, it can no longer do certain things
4) these things were vital to education (this must be presumed, since it is not said)

5) therefore the educational crisis has religious and theological aspects (this must be presumed, since it is unsaid)

As the paragraph now stands, a reader cannot readily follow points one through five. He hasn't been prepared for it. A bridging, linking sentence is needed immediately after the first one. Something like: "The church cannot give education the kind of support it once did"; or, "Education no longer receives from religion and theology the kind of support that once it did." Admittedly, those are awkward (so is the whole thing); they are nonetheless the shoehorns we need.

Of course, it would be even better to begin all over again. The religious dimensions of the educational crisis just can't be dealt with in a single paragraph. The writer desperately needs to find a "plug."

### The out-of-context blues

Another matter we need to find out about our communication: Do a lot of the sentences stand alone, needing no context? Can they be moved around in almost any sequence and still say approximately the same thing? If so, we're probably not dropping bread crumbs.

Here is a paragraph from the back of a church bulletin:

63

> Education is a crucial force and function in our society that demands increased attention from all persons and institutions. More than one-fourth of our population is now enrolled in some form of education. Approximately seven million persons are currently enrolled in higher education institutions.

Although the sentences appear in this order, they could come in any sequence. Sentence one says something in and of itself apart from sentences two and three. Sentence two says something in and of itself apart from one and three. Sentence three says something apart from one and two. When they're put together, they don't lead anywhere. The reader feels like the movie-goer who is shown clouds, more clouds and then clouds again. He's ready to wrap up his popcorn and go.

Some people communicate this way because they have been stung by being quoted out of context. Afraid that it will happen again, they adopt an everything-is-everything style. They fashion sentences so overburdened with their meaning that no one phrase can be slipped out of place and used against them. But that is the coward's way out.

When an opponent misreads or distorts your clear meaning, the onus rests on him. Dr. Percival Hunt, renowned professor of English at the University of Pittsburgh, reminds us, "Writing takes *two* persons to create it." The reader, he insists, "must be able to receive what the writer gives." He must "catch the resonance of association and follow it out, creating the whole from the little."[3]

So, tell us something. Not all at once or over and over again. Tell us something and then tell us something else. And then something else. Keep opening up that vista for your readers or listeners sentence by sentence, paragraph by paragraph. Keep dropping bread crumbs and we will follow.

No one writes all he has to
say, . . . all he is seeing and feeling
and imagining and understanding; all he
holds within the main attempt. He never
could give it all, and he never needs
or wants to try that possibility. He
selects; and there stands his world.

—*Percival Hunt*

# 6.

# *Stick to*

# *Your Guns*

Once you have narrowed your topic, stick to it. Tell the truth at hand and don't worry about the aspects you must, of necessity, neglect. Tell your side or your view, but don't feel obligated to tell all sides, all views. Don't try to offer a "pro" for every "con" or a "vice" for every "versa."

Does this give you qualms? Are we back to the problem posed in chapter 1? Are you worried about short-changing truth? Don't be. Communication is not a pristine art. The very process of turning ideas or experiences into words reduces them and, in so doing, reduces the truth of them. Anne Morrow Lindbergh explains it this way:

> To write or speak is almost inevitably to lie a little. It is an attempt to clothe an intangible in a tangible form; to compress an immeasurable into a mold. And in the act of compression, how Truth is mangled and torn! The writer is the eternal Procrustes who must fit his unhappy guests, his ideas, to his set bed of words. And in the process, it is inevitable that the ideas have their legs chopped off, or pulled out of joint, in order to fit the rigid frame.[1]

It is, indeed, inevitable. We want to be engaged in a perfect activity and produce purity. We want to weld truth so tightly and unmistakably into our utterances that they can never come apart. But we can't. As with the strivings after all other ideals, we do the best we can. With what we've got.

### It's impact that counts

And what we've got are inadequate words, a restless audience and intense competition. In such a situation, truth is served to a higher degree by impact than by totality. We see it in several ways.

Alexander Solzhenitsyn, the Russian novelist and Nobel prize-winner, says, "Those works of art which have scooped up the truth and presented it to us as a living force—they take hold of us, compel us, and nobody ever, not even in ages to come, will appear to refute them."[2] Note that he uses the verb "scooped." Not shoveled. Not bulldozed. A scoop or "wedge" can indeed "be presented to us as a living force." Anything beyond that dies.

We witness its death in reviews like this one of *Emile Durkheim: His Life and Work* in the *New York Times Book Review:*

> One wants more than thoroughness from a scholar; one wants to sense the tensions at play in the intellectual life of his subject. One wants, for example, more than a list of the eight possible meanings of Durkheim's ambiguous distinction between . . . ; one wants to know what was at stake in each of the. . . . One wants a balanced account, to be sure, but not if balance has to be achieved at the cost of movement.[3]

One wants more thoroughness, the reviewer says and, interestingly enough, means *less* than thoroughness. Just because you know "eight possible meanings" doesn't justify unloading them. "No one writes all he has to say," declares Dr. Hunt. No one spreads out "all he is seeing and feeling and imagining and understanding; all he holds within the main attempt. He never could give it all, and he never needs or wants to try that possibility. He selects; and there stands his world."

## Liberation

Once a communicator understands all this, he is set free. He can pick and choose without feeling guilty about what he must, perforce, leave out. He can write and speak directly to his own point, not hedging, equivocating or playing nursemaid to a lot of "on the other hands." He can create the kind of terse, concentrated "wedges" that make an impact. He needn't clutter his sentences with apologies for oversimplifying; oversimplifying is the name of the game.

He doesn't have to scurry after trivial contradictions. I have a newspaper column entitled "Some Things That Are Old Fashioned." The writer begins:

> In these days of TV, pushbutton phones, jet air travel and space ships, old-fashioned things are pretty much forgotten except on special occasions and celebrations.

What would happen if he began:

> In these days of TV, pushbutton phones, jet air travel and space ships, old-fashioned things are pretty much forgotten.

Would someone come up to him the next day, slap him on the shoulder and demand, "But what about those special occasions and celebrations?" I doubt it.

He continues:

> Have you ever stopped to think that certain things in the modern world are absolutely unchanged? Customs change, ideas change, but some things are positively unchangeable. The following things have defied every effort of man to change them.

What would be lost if he left out the second sentence? Only ten additional words that derail the thought. For here is a would-be communicator who keeps working against himself. He is striving (we hope) toward some point about forgotten, changeless things and all along the way he brings up: (a) occasions when they *are* remembered, and (b) things that *do* change. Bureaucrats call that "being counterproductive."

The liberated communicator doesn't have to pursue "other sides." He realizes that the world does this for us. As soon as any point of view surfaces (makes its impact), contrary views do too. That's the way mankind operates. As soon as one person arises and insists, "This is true," another arises to counter with "No, it isn't." For every columnist who writes about "What Is Old Fashioned" there is one who writes about "What Is Modern."

Partisanship breeds partisanship. And each partisan does better with his own contention. Whenever anyone tries to handle both sides of an argument or all sides, he runs two risks: that he will be unfair by slighting the side(s) with which he disagrees and/or that he will lose his potential receivers by assigning himself more than he can handle in a way that they will take.

## Fairness to his side

When he is relieved of the burden of being fair to all sides, the communicator can be fair to his own side. Fatigue no longer winnows his sentences. Instead, his purpose, like a command helicopter, hovers over his efforts, accepting and rejecting words on the basis of how well each serves the cause. This intense selectivity molds his material into the "living force" Solzhenitsyn praised. It produces passages that take hold of us, compel us and move us.

See the difference, if you will, in two paragraphs dealing with the same subject matter. The first is Dan Collins's, describing the birth of his son. We have already noted in chapter 3 that, although he had a stated purpose (to acquaint us with his son), he didn't adhere to it. Instead he tried to reconstruct the total experience and, as he went along, his tiredness determined what he included and what he left out. He wrote:

One Tuesday night at 11:48 my wife awakened me. Expectantly she exclaimed, "Our little guest will soon be here. We must rush to the hospital to meet him." Arriving too early, we were forced to wait for several hours. My resentment kindled as painful cries arose from the labor room. Meanwhile my anticipation of new life could hardly be contained. The hours seemed as days, but finally the climax came. The nurse announced that within seconds we would be a family. Then I was so caught up in the whole miracle of birth that I forgot my fear and resentment. "Is he a boy?" I asked anxiously. "What is his weight? Does he have a strong cry? Will he be healthy?"

Contrast this with William Gibson's description in *Mass for the Dead*. The author's purpose is to show that "the coming of children is a birth in us also . . . and with every birth the tale (of humanity) begins anew." He writes:

It was a rainy dawn when I escorted my waddling wife into a hospital lobby, and three hours later I saw the tiny creature who had dwelt so long and anonymously in her womb: at the elevator a masked nurse bearing him from delivery to maternity waved me back, but lifted the cloth so that I could spy the squeezed face and dark hair still matted with his mother's blood, and at last something in me found its pedalpoint. By what stumblings in the dark his mother and I had come to that beginning is another story, part and not part of this, but I had been a long way around and was home. Diminutive head, it pulled like magnetic bone at everything in my life; work, marriage, conscience, all was changed.[4]

Gibson's paragraph got a hearing in a widely read book. It made the necessary impact. Collins's never saw the light of day.

### Encounter the test

Truth, I repeat, is served to a greater degree by impact than by totality. For it is at its point of destination that its reliability emerges. In Pearl Harbor rather than the Pentagon. In the marketplace rather than the library. In the rough-and-tumble of life rather than the placid cloister. It holds up or crumbles in encounter. For this reason the Supreme Court will not render decisions on theoretical possibilities. If a person is contemplating an action and isn't sure whether it's constitutional, he can't sidle up to the judges and ask their opinions on the side. They will listen only to two sides locked in a genuine controversy. For surely it is out of such a crucible that the purest truth emerges.

No one, then, can weld reality literally and actually into a combination of words. It's "out there" beyond us. We can only fit our words to what we see (or what we are given to see) and let the other fellow do the same. He will, if you will. So go ahead. Dive into your truth. Tell your side. Do your thing. And stick to your guns.

He who knows himself to be
profound endeavors to be clear; he
who would like to appear profound
to the crowd endeavors to be obscure.

—*Friedrich Nietzsche*

## Beetle Bailey ® By Mort Walker

# 7.

# Call a

# Spade a Shovel

Do your thing, yes, but don't forget the people. Keep in mind your purpose, but also keep in mind your listeners/readers. You don't want to con them, bore them or put them off. You will remember that it takes only a split second to switch a channel, snap shut a book or, as Billy Wilder said, wrap up the popcorn and go home! Therefore you want to communicate as one human being to another. Not with jargon that makes the one who doesn't understand it feel like an outsider. And not with high-blown language to impress.

At the outset of World War II an aide sent this memo to President Roosevelt's desk:

> Such preparations shall be made as will completely obscure all Federal Buildings occupied by the federal government during an air raid for any period of time from visibility by reason of external or internal illumination. Such obscuration may be obtained either by blackout construction or by termination of illumination. This will, of course, require that in building areas in which production must continue during the blackout, construction must be provided so that internal illumination may continue. Other areas may be obscured by terminating the illumination.

Mr. Roosevelt revised it:

> Tell them that in buildings where they have to keep the work going, they should put something across the window. In buildings where they can afford to let the work stop for awhile, they should turn out the lights!

Stay down to earth. Or prepare to be found out. Like Michael Rossman who wrote a 363-page book called *On Learning and Social Change* (two huge subjects). He filled it with all sorts of research, charts and diagrams. Then along came Jan Berry. Reviewing it in the *Washington Post,* he said:

> And for all his pomp and circumstance, Rossman's major insights can be boiled down to two: People learn best in small groups, from each other, doing something they consider substantial rather than make-believe; and technology can be a powerful help-mate rather than a daily horror, if people would only learn that they are not impotent before the mysteries of machines.[1]

Bingo, in one sentence an upstart journalist who knew how to get to the heart of a matter reduced the tome to naught! Friedrich Nietzsche left us this gem: "He who knows himself to be profound endeavors to be clear; he who would like to appear profound to the crowd endeavors to be obscure."

### Fashion a new net

Use ordinary language. But don't be content with an ordinary presentation. Draw a fresh bead on your topic and tell it in some new way. If truth cannot be welded to a page anyway, you aren't honor bound to come at it head-on. If it's "out there," you're free to fashion whatever net you can in which to catch it: humor, dialogue, fantasy, satire, drama—anything. The Navy almost did it with a warning—the

83

one it sent to Pearl Harbor just before the attack.

And do you remember Nathan? The Lord sent him to rebuke King David for murdering Uriah and "appropriating" his wife. So what did Nathan do? He stood before David and began:

> There were two men in a certain city, the one rich and the other poor. The rich man had very many flocks and herds; but the poor man had nothing but one little ewe lamb, which he had bought. And he brought it up, and it grew up with him and with his children; it used to eat of his morsel, and drink from his cup, and lie in his bosom, and it was like a daughter to him. Now there came a traveler to the rich man, and he was unwilling to take one of his own flock or herd to prepare for the wayfarer who had come to him, but he took the poor man's lamb, and prepared it for the man who had come to him.

Going on, we read:

> Then David's anger was greatly kindled against the man; and he said to Nathan, "As the Lord lives, the man who has done this deserves to die; and he shall restore the lamb fourfold, because he did this thing, and because he had no pity."
> Nathan said to David, "You are the man!" (2 Sam. 12:1–7).

In the passage that follows (vv. 7–12), Nathan proceeds to identify the rich man as David, the poor man as Uriah and the ewe lamb as Bathsheba. At the end, David breaks down and confesses, "I have sinned against the Lord." Would the dialogue ever have arrived at that satisfactory ending, if Nathan had stomped in and, at the outset, accused David of adultery and murder? I doubt it.

## Use your imagination

Let your imagination loose on your topic. Try to see it from a unique angle. Children are very good at this, because they come to experience without our preconceived notions. Teaching children, being around them, reading books of their sayings or letters or watching TV shows featuring their creative efforts can often give us fresh slants.

I like the story of the little girl whose mother took her to visit a farm for the first time. The two of them explored the barn, the hen house and the various pens. At the conclusion the mother asked her what she liked best. And she answered, "The six little pigs blowing up the big pig!" Well, Sister Corita looked at a cereal box with its cheery greeting, "The best to you each morning," and created a new religious art. Marshall McLuhan looked at high school dropouts and saw them, in our electronic age, as a jump

85

ahead of everybody instead of one behind. And recently someone, somewhere, looked at a beanbag, saw it enlarged and, *voilà*—a legless chair!

Foreigners, outsiders and recent converts of various sorts can help us with our vision. I once took a German girl to an American baseball game. During the first few innings I explained what was going on out on the field and felt she understood. But in the last half of the eighth, the batter got a single and I began yelling, "He got a base! He got a base!" Suddenly my companion's eyes lighted up and she exclaimed, "Oh, you mean those little pillows!"

### Keep freshness coming

Keep freshness coming into your life. Read new books as well as old; see new plays and movies, sculpture and art; listen to new songs and poetry; play some new games. Don't restrict yourself to one field of interest only or one set of friends. From time to time read the house organ of some business or industry other than your own. If you're a minister, read the magazine of another denomination. If you're a lawyer, read a prison newspaper. If you're a poet, read a book on engineering, and, if you're an engineer, read a book of poems. If you go back to school for a "refresher" course, sign up for something different from or only parallel to your line of work. Travel occasionally, even if it's only crosstown to see "how the other half lives." Keep open to changing ideas and keep learning: a new language, a new skill, a new way of getting to work in the morning or a new tune to whistle.

Play around with unlikely combinations. If you run across a quiz entitled "Are You Fun to Be With?" give it in your imagination to a John Calvin or Ralph Nader. Go through *Time* or *Newsweek* magazine and substitute captions related to your occupation for those already under the pictures. Imagine interviewing Barbara Walters about farm equipment or Peter Fonda about trends in African basket-weaving. Throw a dream (or possibly nightmare) party and compose a guest list of people who would otherwise never get together. What would they say to each other? Who wouldn't speak to whom? What games would they play? Refuse to play? Match up several pairs of people solely on the basis of their names and concoct conversations between them, like Julia *Child* and Victor *Mature,* Harry *Golden* and Ringo *Starr,* Billie Jean *King* and Steve McQueen, or Norman Vincent *Peale* and Linda *Blair.*

Finally, practice making something new out of something old. Update the nursery rhymes. (On TV's "Sesame Street" Little Miss Muffet now sits on a waterbed, eats crunchy Granola and refuses to flee from any mere spider.) How would Red Riding Hood or The Boy Who Cried "Wolf" shape up today? If you're a minister, clothe some of your favorite Bible

87

passages in your *own* words. You need not read them from the pulpit, but you need not be afraid or ashamed to, either. C. C. Jung says, "Eternal truth needs a *human language* that alters with the spirit of the time."

Yes, a human language, spoken as one ordinary mortal to another, carrying with it the freshness and spirit of the times. Communicate humanly. Call a spade a shovel.

"Consider this a warning of war."
—Navy cablegram, November 1941

# 8.

# Squeeze, Please

Writer Mary Shideler defines truth as "the facts as fully as is required for conveying their important implications."[1] *More* than that fails truth, as we have seen. If war is imminent, our cablegrams must say, "Consider this a warning of war." If a poster is all our potential receiver will take, we create the most provocative poster we can. We work with wedges, not totalities. We try to keep our ideas from drowning in a sea of words.

But we need not belabor the need for brevity.

91

Rather, we need to learn to shorten and tighten our prose.

## Use those verbs

How? To begin with, hire lots of verbs. Strong, vigorous, colorful verbs. Then put them to work. They're wonderful; they explain, demonstrate, explore, investigate, declare, assert and even shout and scream for us. And best of all, they blot and squeeze. They can absorb all sorts of inconsequential clutter-words. A seminary student had this sentence in a practice sermon:

> For this is the point at which we usually become
> edgy in these discipleship passages in the New
> Testament, and the preacher usually relieves
> us by saying that money just happened to
> be this young man's problem, implying that my
> problem in accepting fully this new life
> couldn't be so drastic.

Fifty-one words! It wouldn't fit on a poster. I edited it to:

> We grow edgy when we hear the New Testament
> demands of discipleship. The preacher,
> sensing our uneasiness, purrs that money just
> happened to be this young man's barrier.
> My roadblock, he implies, springs from something
> far less drastic.

Thirty-eight words broken into three sentences. The verb "grow" soaks up "usually become"; "purrs" absorbs "relieves by saying" and "springs" takes in "couldn't be."

With different verbs, see what we can do for one of the paragraphs in the letter quoted in chapter 2:

Original:

> In the town of _____, a Sunday school had been held among the adults in the house of a Christian family. However, a vacation Bible school brought in many children, making it necessary to have a regular Sunday school for the children also. This was managed by an earlier hour on Sunday afternoon so that there would be sufficient time to reach the other Sunday school in _____.

Total words: 68.

Revised:

> In the town of _____, the adult Sunday school continues in the house of a Christian family. However, a vacation Bible school attracted many children, so we launched a regular Sunday school for them as well. It convenes early Sunday afternoon, giving me sufficient time to reach the other school in _____.

Total words: 52.

93

Active verbs squeeze out sixteen clutter-words, all the while improving the sense of what is said!

Keep the verb "to be" (and its forms *is, are, was* and *were*) in the bone pile. Draw it out, à la dominoes, *only* when all other possibilities prove unworkable. "Is" seems small and innocuous, but it brings with it a boring retinue. When it becomes your sole choice, try to buttress it with other verbs and verb-forms of substance. Olov Hartman does it like this in *Holy Masquerade:*

> It is [main verb] eerie, for one *knows* that the
> differences that *have been waved* away so
> hastily and *have disappeared will come stealing*
> back like ghosts, *hide* themselves in closets,
> and *roll* skulls in the attic at night.[2]

Search your mind for strong verbs to carry the essence of your message and fortify weak ones whenever you can.

### Beware—

Certain sentences by their very structure telegraph ahead that they are going to be too long. These words are clues to spotting them:

| the | this | is |
|-----|------|-------|
| it | that | thing |

When they appear *in clusters,* alarms ought to go off and buzzers sound. For when you say, for example,

> The reason for this is that . . .
> Or: The cause for this is that . . .

you've said six words and haven't yet gotten to any substance. If the cause or reason is the least bit complicated, the chance is high that you will load the sentence with more freight than the reader can take.
When you say

> The important thing about this is that . . .
> Or: The interesting thing about this is that . . .

you've said *seven* words and haven't arrived at substance. Ditto

> It is important to realize that this . . .
> And: It is important to recognize that this . . .

You've peppered the receiver with *nine* say-nothing words when you begin

> There is every reason to believe that this is . . .

In nine cases out of ten, alternatives for these structures can be found. For instance, if you've gotten to a place where you want to say

> The reason for this is that . . .

you've come to a place where you can simply ask
"Why?" Then, in a new sentence (or several subsequent sentences) give the reason:

> In 1974 Richard M. Nixon resigned as President
> of the United States. The reason for this
> action was that . . .

> In 1974 Richard M. Nixon resigned as President
> of the United States. Why? Because he
> covered up . . .

We have already noted that we can on occasions
omit either the subject or the predicate in certain
sentences. Sometimes we can cast part of a declarative sentence in question form and save words. Exclamations and imperatives help too. Instead of
saying

> This obligation is important in that . . .
> Try: Accept this obligation [imperative]. You
> will discover . . .

If the discovery sounds significant, you will have com-
municated the importance of the responsibility *more*
powerfully than if you had stated it outright. (When
people tell me blatantly that something is important,
I tend to believe it isn't.)

### Put on the brakes

96      There are a couple of other ways of putting the

brakes on runaway sentences. Encompassing phrases help. I have a copy of a speech given verbatim by an electronics expert several years ago. He is pointing out and demonstrating various pieces of audio-visual equipment. From time to time he says, "The interesting thing about this is" (or "these are"). Then he invariably tries to stuff too much into the rest of the line:

> The interesting thing about the language laboratories is that there weren't any about seven years ago and there are a lot of them now and that is complicated equipment.

> The interesting part about the Craig Reader is that they use the filmstrip animated to a piece of plastic and it's about the size of a 12-inch ruler.

> What is really interesting about that is you can talk English into that and turn the dial over to French and it will type out French.

When you have said "The interesting thing about the ——— is," you have reached the *brink* of a complete thought. (A sentence by definition expresses a complete thought.) All you need is a word or phrase large enough to encompass "what is interesting" and you can stop. A subsequent sentence or two can break down and elucidate the word or phrase. Here's how it would work with those above:

The interesting thing about the language

laboratory is their *rapid growth*. Several
years ago . . .

The interesting feature of the Craig Reader is its
*automation*. With a filmstrip the size of a 12-inch
ruler . . .

What is really interesting about the voice-writer
is its versatility. Speak English into the mouth-
piece, turn the dial to French . . .

The braking phrase makes the rest of the material
more manageable.

## Double-feel

Sometimes such a phrase can be made up or coined.
It need not be immediately comprehensible to the
reader/listener, since upcoming sentences will clarify
it. Here's how William F. Kraft does it in *A Psychology of Nothingness:*

Most normal people have difficulty making
sense of their nothingness. A conventional negative approach toward nothingness can be called
"double-feel." Double-feel simply involves a feeling
about a feeling; a person becomes depressed about
being depressed, anxious about being anxious,
frustrated with his frustration, bored with being
bored, guilty about his loneliness. Double-feel
means that a person cannot accept what he really
feels, or that he feels that what he does feel is
negative or is a sign of something negative.[3]

98

We don't understand "double-feel" when we first encounter it, but it enables Kraft to end sentence two in ten words, a desirable length. Here is another example from Dr. Donald MacKay, speaking on the TV show "Firing Line":

> But, you see, that doesn't get away from the fallacy. I give it the general name of "nothing but-ery." The no smoking sign is nothing but ink on cardboard, so we'll go on smoking. Talk about B. F. Skinner as a man is nothing but talk about a piece of meat of a certain size wobbling up and down emitting sound waves so I'll ignore his views, or at least I'll only calculate what I can do to the nervous system by emitting sound waves in return. This "nothing but-ery" is fallacious.

How much better to be temporarily confused over the coined "double-feel" or "nothing-but-ery" than forever lost in a morass of words! The British cleric J.B. Phillips had a field day with this method in his book *Your God Is Too Small*. He describes various inadequate (too small) concepts of God. When he believes his description is clear, he labels the "god" under discussion (the Grand Old Man, the Second-hand god, the Third-Programme god, the God-of-escape). Once the concept is labeled, the author goes on to discuss its inadequacies. Thus "God-in-a-box" becomes a kind of shorthand understood by both the writer and the reader, sparing both of them many extra words.

## No length, then?

Are all long constructions then absolutely taboo? No, but they should be put in *by design*. They should help create a desired effect. Here is playwright Neil Simon writing autobiographically:

> I grow. An inch here, an inch there, a crack in the voice, a stubble on the chin, a passing shot at puberty, a glancing blow at sex and Shazam, I'm a man. If not a man, at least a tall boy. Would you accept an enormous child? My dreams, my goals, my ambitions are to be like Them, the Others. Accepted, Respected and Noticed.

In the second sentence he deals with a long period of time via a long sentence.

Dan Collins missed a similar opportunity. Writing about his stint in the waiting room, he said, "The hours seemed as days, but finally the climax came." An accomplished writer would have put a period after "days." Then he would have helped us *feel* the burden of those hours with something like: "I gazed steadily at the clock, watching to see either hand make even the slightest move that would assure me time had not decided on this night of nights to stand stock still."

Write long sentences to depict something long; a complicated one to depict something intricate. But ordinarily, keep sentences short (ten to fifteen words) and simple.

Eliminate all such phrases as "I think," "I hold," "I am convinced," "I believe." Your audience/readers will assume that you are sharing your convictions with them unless you state otherwise. Eliminate wishy-washy terms like "perhaps," "maybe," "possibly," "probably," "usually," "sometimes" and "somewhat." Don't make *any* reference whatsoever to how little time or space you have been given. And don't offer apologies for why you expect to do (or are doing) a poor job of communicating.

Watch out for "real" and "really." The phrase "in a very real sense" means nothing. To describe people as real heroes, real Christians, real dog-lovers or real whatevers accomplishes nothing that the nouns by themselves (heroes, Christians, dog-lovers) don't do. To insist that a person is really innocent or really dedicated or really profound tends to arouse the suspicion that he isn't (really).

Eliminate:

> It is obvious that
> I need not tell you
> Everyone knows
> You know
> It goes without saying
> As a matter of fact
> That fact is that
> As I was saying

Rarely, if ever
Actually.

Squeeze your sentences dry of empty phrases. We need the facts only as fully as required for conveying their important implications.

Train your mind to think:

Man bites dog.
Not: The dog was bitten by the man.

# THE FAMILY CIRCUS    By Bil Keane

4-3

"A pronoun is for when you don't know the noun's
name."

# 9.

# Goof-proofing

● *Never use a fifty-cent word when a ten-cent word will do.* Call up any long or technical words you need to do the job, but don't use them to show off or dissemble. I have a tract on Women's Lib written by a seminary student. It is fraught with such terms as *paradigms, social customs, structures* and *critical reflection.* The writer is trying to be very scholarly. But she's really just putting a lot of "in" words together without close attention to what she's assembling.

At one point she asks, "Do I live . . . by the quiet acceptance of the false ultimates of conspicuous and subtly discriminatory laws and social stereotypes?" The entire question is twenty-nine words long, and the last half (which I am quoting) is out of control. Does "conspicuous" modify "laws" or "discriminatory laws"? If "laws," what does it mean: what are "conspicuous laws"? If "discriminatory laws," should it not be "conspicuous*ly*"? Can laws be both "conspicuously" discriminatory and "subtly" so? Yes, the discrimination can be expressed in a veiled manner but appear naked and blatant to the wronged party. But this is almost too much freight for one sentence; it certainly shouldn't be jammed into a portion of one that's already overloaded!

Germaine Greer, who was a Commonwealth Scholar at Cambridge and has a doctorate from Newham, also writes about Women's Lib. And she uses such terms as *paradigms, structures* and *critical reflection* (she speaks of a woman "reassessing herself"). But here is a sentence which, in its flavor, is typical of what we find in *The Female Eunuch:*

> The mousy secretary blossoms into the feminine stereotype when she reddens her lips, lets down her hair and puts on something frilly.[1]

Who is the scholar? Who is the communicator?

## A "now" feeling

● *Use present tense whenever possible.* It gives a "now" feeling that Americans like. And verbs uncluttered by a lot of *was*es and *were*s, *have*s and *had*s come on stronger. Oftimes the tense of verbs, especially in subordinate clauses, doesn't matter. In such cases, opt for the present. Consider:

Thales *arose* as the first man in history who *perceived* that there *was* an order in nature [past].

Or: Thales *arises* as the first man in history to *perceive* that there *is* an order in nature [present].

Sometimes a present tense "situation" can be manipulated. Wilma Dykeman does it with skill in *Return the Innocent Earth.*[2] In chapter 13 she uses the storyteller's reminiscences about his father to ease the reader into a series of now incidents:

Chapter begins on page 284:
    My father was a voice: calm, firm, edged with steel and kindness. And a hand: warm, secure, leading and loosening. And a glance: tolerant but perceptive beyond comfort.
    I remember the voice.
    It *is* [present] an afternoon in October. Sunlight *falls* around me and over the porch. . . .

Introduction to new section on page 288:
I remember his hand.

**107**

> The midwinter day *is* cold and we *are* in the mountains. . . .

> Introduction to new section on page 292:
> I remember my father's look.
> It *is* another year. Five years. The heat of mid-summer *seals* the early evening in a breathless quiet. . . .

### Active voice preferred

• *Prefer active to passive voice.* Train your mind to think:

> Man bites dog.
> Not: The dog was bitten by the man.

The latter leads to deviousness almost without our knowing it. Donald Hall speaks of "using the passive mood to attribute to no one in particular opinions that one is unwilling to call one's own." [3] People also use it to create the impression that they're saying something of substance when they aren't. They often deceive themselves, as I think the committee did that composed this:

> The term *crisis* is used because while in the past questions have been raised about various aspects of the school system, today the whole structure and establishment are being challenged and it is felt we are approaching a critical juncture in edu-

cational history when as a society we will be faced with decisive alternatives.

When we "de-passify" that, it comes out:

> Our committee terms this a crisis. In the past experts have called into question various aspects of the school system. But today they are challenging the whole structure and establishment. We are approaching a critical juncture where we will face decisive alternatives.

Sound punctured? It is. While the verbs acted on the subjects, my mind had to keep arcing back and forth. This yo-yoing slowed me down and created the illusion that I was plowing through something significant. But when the verbs act on objects, I find that *I* only faced with "decisive alternatives"; I'm faced with them all the time. Since they're never spelled out, I can't get excited about the so-called crisis.

### Contrasts and comparisons

• *Keep contrasting and comparing material in close juxtaposition.* When we want to measure the respective heights of two children, what do we do? We put them *back to back*. Many people weaken their comparison by putting them too far apart. They run all the description of A, then all the description of A-1 and ask *us* to do the matching.

In a sermon he preached to his fellow seminarians, a student told of having a conversation with a friend who was a sculptor. And then he said:

And as a student of the Bible, I could assure my friend that what he had just said was perfectly parallel to the eternal life God gives us: the best part is the satisfaction of studying each situation intimately, and then, knowledgeable of eternal law, to make each stroke with the finest care, with the greatest creative freedom we possess— and with the added assurance that the finished product is secure in His craftsmanship.

Here is the comparison he was trying to convey—the one that dribbled away because his hearers couldn't successfully juggle so many items so far apart:

What my friend said parallels the way *we* live. He studied the marble; we study our situations. He knew the laws of artistry; we know the laws of God. His satisfaction sprang from the venture itself. So does ours. Like him, we make each action —each "stroke"—with the finest care, with all the creative freedom we possess. And the finished product? It stands secure in . . .

### Pronouns and antecedents

● *Keep pronouns close to their antecedents.* Either immediately before:

As the crewman threw *him* overboard, *Jonah* yelled, "Help!"

or just after:

As the crewman threw Jonah overboard, he yelled, "Help!"

But never with another word intervening with which I might mistakenly match it:

As the *crewman* threw Jonah overboard, *he* yelled, "Heave ho."

### Descriptive phrases and clauses

● *Keep all descriptive phrases and clauses as close as possible to what they are describing.* Here's what happens to an episode from Acts 20, when they stray:

Being an evangelist, we can imagine that Paul preached whenever he got a chance. [Are "we" an evangelist or is "Paul"?] Preaching once in an upper room to a crowd that was tired, you can understand what happened to one in the group. [Who was preaching?] Sitting in the window, as Paul talked on and on, he fell asleep. [Paul did?] And as Paul was about to pronounce the benediction, the crowd saw him lean back and fall from the window. [Everything clear?] Immediately they rushed down the stairs and, because he

111

wasn't breathing, Paul went down too. [And that's hard to do!] Throwing himself down on him, he began to revive and stir. [Still clear?] After everybody was assured that he was breathing again, Paul offered the benediction! [Breath is important to benedictions.]

### Matching number and person

● *Be meticulously sure that pronouns match their antecedents in number and person.* How often we get this kind of confusion:

Angry citizens protested to the city council. As a result, they rescinded the ordinance.

Correctly, "they" can refer only to the "citizens." Technically, then, the sentence indicates that government broke down and mob rule took over. But did it? Or did the communicator just forget that a "council" is an "it"? So is an assembly, a congress, a department, a church, a group, and committee. We can refer to "the members" of one of these bodies as "they," but not the body itself.

Disagreements in number occur frequently too:

*Every* alien living in the United States is required to register his address with the government in January, regardless of whether *they* have been here a short time or several years.

"Every" is singular and thus each reference to him/
her must be singular:

> *Every* alien is required . . . regardless of whether
> *he* has been . . .

Or the shift must be completely to the plural:

> *All* aliens are required . . . regardless of whether
> *they* have been. . . .

## Easy with the adjectives and adverbs

• *Use adjectives and adverbs sparingly.* Joyce
Maynard, you remember (chapter 1), wasn't interested in reading descriptions of people's eyes or their
sitting rooms or the sunsets they walked through.
Don't pile on repetitions; if it's "colossal," we'll assume that it's also "stupendous." Writing that de-
pends on a lot of adjectives and adverbs sounds
flowery and fake.

> He extended his *loving* arms and in a *gentle*
> voice with *pleading* petition invited them into
> his *humble* shelter.

It can also get very complicated, like this Niebuhr
sentence:

> It is *not easy* to understand that the *perennial*

113

> problems of man's existence in history will re-
> appear on *every* level of *historical* achievement
> in a period when the changes in the conditions of
> his life are *so great* as to create the illusion that
> *new* conditions and achievements have eliminated
> the *perennial* problems.[4]

It is also not easy to understand why anyone would compose a sentence like that! Yours will come out better if you goof-proof them by observing the guideposts staked out in this chapter.

What I have written,
I have written.

—*Pontius Pilate*

# 10.

# End Before

# Your Ending

Without deliberate restraint, we begin *before* our beginning. We insist on correcting a trivial mistake made by the person introducing us instead of wading into our speech. Or we tell a couple of irrelevant jokes or dredge up some unnecessary "background."

Likewise, without deliberate restraint, we end *after* our ending. Paul Scherer pictures preachers who talk on and on and says, "They make you think of a baker with sticky dough on his hands. They just cannot get

117

rid of it." [1] And preachers aren't alone; we all filibuster at times.

### Trust your receivers

We find it hard to trust our receivers. We don't believe them when they tell us flat out, as the *Post* reader quoted in chapter 5 did, that they love to make connections, decipher events and ferret out the communicator's meaning. So in our skepticism we *tell* them. We explain, "This means that . . ." or, "The lesson we learn from this is . . . ." We become, in effect, our receivers' brain, forgetting that they have their own and we ought to be, instead, their sensory radar.

Consider this stewardship appeal that appeared in a denominational magazine:

> Once upon a time there was a man who had nothing. And God gave him ten apples. He gave him three apples to eat; He gave him three apples to trade for a shelter from the sun and rain; He gave him three apples to trade for clothing to wear; He gave him one apple so that he might have something to give back to God to show his gratitude.
>
> The man ate three apples; he traded three for a shelter from the sun and rain; he traded three for clothing to wear; then he looked at the tenth apple. It seemed bigger and juicier than the rest. So the man ate the tenth apple and gave back to God . . . the core.

I wish I could say that here it ended. But it didn't. The writer continued:

> God has given you enough apples to supply your needs—plus one with which you may show your gratitude to him. The choice is yours. Will you return to God the largest and juiciest of your apples—or only the core?

Every time we sit down to compose, caution draws up a chair. We're so afraid someone will miss our point or misinterpret the wedge that we overtell. We become super-explainers and, before we know it, simple paragraphs turn into encyclopedias. Pilate understood the process well. You remember that he had a sign nailed on Jesus' cross that read "King of the Jews." But an editorial committee of Pharisees asked him to change it. Don't write, the committee said, "King of the Jews," but "This man said 'I am King of the Jews.'" Pilate saw that if he did, he would probably have to put up a huge billboard to handle all the other "additions" and "clarifications" the committee would then want. So he nipped it in the bud with, "What I have written, I have written!"

## Shed light

Scripps-Howard newspapers are issued under the motto, "Shed light and the people will find a way." I commend this as a guide to concluding. When you

119

have shed light, stop! Alvin Toffler (who began well) does it in *Future Shock:*

> . . . the basic thrust of this book is diagnosis. For diagnosis precedes cure, and we cannot begin to help ourselves until we become sensitively conscious of the problem. These pages will have served their purpose if, in some measure, they help create the consciousness needed for man to undertake the control of change, the guidance of his evolution. For, by making imaginative use of change to channel change, we cannot only spare ourselves the trauma of future shock, we can reach out and humanize distant tomorrows.[2]

The reader is on his own to think of ways to use "change to channel change." At the end of the fantastic *Cat in the Hat,* the TV viewer must himself decide whether to "tell mother."

Of course, not all conclusions need to be so open-ended. They only need to be appropriate to their contexts. They can tell us the butler did it if it's highly unlikely that we can figure it out. An end can tie up loose ends and bump off the villains. It can summarize and tally. It can have a twist that surprises, as *How to Be Your Own Best Friend* does. The patient-questioner asks, "I feel that I have learned many secrets from you, and heard many wise words. I hope I can remember them." And the team answers, "Of course you'll remember them; you knew them all the time."[3] Imagine what would have happened if I'd seen that before I bought the book!

Usually, however, endings match the material. Could any sentence be more fitting to draw to a close William Shirer's best-selling epic than "But the Third Reich has passed into history"?[4] Or any better way be found to end the Twenty-Third Psalm than "I shall dwell in the house of the Lord forever"?

## Do whatever needs doing

Good endings do whatever needs doing. They round off what needs to be rounded off and leave hanging whatever has yet to be explored or resolved. Anne Morrow Lindbergh does a little of each in the last paragraph of *Gift from the Sea:*

> The waves echo behind me. Patience—Faith— Openness, is what the sea has to teach. Simplicity —Solitude—Intermittency. . . . But there are other beaches to explore. There are more shells to find. This is only a beginning.[5]

Just remember to end before

THE END.

# Notes

## Chapter 1

1.  Joyce Maynard, *Looking Back: A Chronicle of Growing Up Old in the Sixties* (New York: Doubleday, 1973), p. 64.

## Chapter 2

1.  Antoine de Saint-Exupéry, *Wind, Sand and Stars* (New York: Harcourt Brace Jovanovich, Inc., 1945), p. 237.

## Chapter 3

1.  Quoted in *New York Times.*
2.  Quoted in *Nashville Tennessean.*
3.  Alvin Toffler, *Future Shock* (New York: Random House, 1970), p. 11.
4.  Ibid., p. 12.
5.  Charles Merrill Smith, *When the Saints Go Marching Out* (New York: Doubleday, 1969), p. 1.
6.  Hans H. Kirst, *What Became of Gunner Asch* (New York: Harper & Row, 1963), p. 1.

7.  Frederick Forsyth, *The Day of the Jackal* (New York: Viking Press, 1971), p. 3.
8.  P. G. Wodehouse, *The Most of Wodehouse* (New York: Simon & Schuster, 1960), p. 316.

## Chapter 4

1.  Sonya Rudikoff's review of *Group Marriage: A Study of Contemporary Multilateral Marriage* by Larry and Joan M. Constantine in "Book World," *Washington Post,* May 6, 1973.
2.  Dorothy Bryant, *Ella Price's Journal* (Philadelphia: J. B. Lippincott Co., 1972), p. 13.
3.  Ibid., pp. 73–74.
4.  Rachel Carson, *The Edge of the Sea* (Boston: Houghton Mifflin Co., 1955), p. 1.

## Chapter 5

1.  Letter to the editor in "Book World," *Washington Post,* April 22, 1973.
2.  Thomas Howard, *An Antique Drum* (Philadelphia: J. B. Lippincott Co., 1969), p. 83.
3.  Percival Hunt, *The Gift of the Unicorn: Essays on Writing* (University of Pittsburgh Press, 1965), p. 51.

## Chapter 6

1.  Anne Lindbergh, *The Wave of the Future* (New York: Harcourt Brace Jovanovich, Inc., 1940), p. 6, 7.

2. Alexander Solzhenitsyn, *Nobel Lecture*, tr. by F. D. Reeve, (New York: Farrar, Straus & Giroux, Inc., 1972), p. 7.
3. From a review by Philip Rosenberg of *Emile Durkheim: His Life and Work*, in *New York Times*, July 15, 1973.
4. William Gibson, *Mass for the Dead* (New York: Atheneum Press, 1968), p. 311.

## Chapter 7

1. Jan Berry, in a review of Michael Rossman, *On Learning and Social Change* (New York: Random House, 1972), in *Washington Post*, August 19, 1972.

## Chapter 8

1. Mary Shideler, "Coup de Grace," *Christian Century*, December 7, 1966.
2. Olov Hartman, *Holy Masquerade* (Grand Rapids: Eerdmans, 1963), p. 33. Used by permission.
3. William F. Kraft, *A Psychology of Nothingness* (Philadelphia: Westminster Press, 1974), p. 136.

## Chapter 9

1. Germaine Greer, *The Female Eunuch* (New York: McGraw-Hill Book Co., 1971), p. 49.
2. Wilma Dykeman, *Return the Innocent Earth* (New York: Holt, Rinehart and Winston, 1973).
3. Donald Hall, *The Modern Stylists: Writers on the Art of Writing* (New York: Macmillan, 1968), p. 6.

4. Reinhold Niebuhr, *The Nature and Destiny of Man* (New York: Charles Scribner's Sons, 1943), p. 181.

**Chapter 10**

1. Paul Scherer, *We Have This Treasure* (New York: Harper & Row, 1944), p. 175.
2. Toffler, *Future Shock*, p. 430.
3. Mildred Newman and Bernard Berkowitz, *How to Be Your Own Best Friend* (New York: Random House, 1973), p. 54.
4. William Shirer, *The Rise and Fall of the Third Reich* (New York: Simon and Shuster, 1960), p. 1, 140.
5. Anne Morrow Lindbergh, *Gift from the Sea* (New York: Random House, 1955), p. 128.